Danny and the Bump-a-lump

Story written by Gill Munton
Illustrated by Tim Archbold

Speed Sounds

Consonants *Ask children to say the sounds.*

f ff ph	l ll le	m mm	n nn (**kn**)	r rr wr	s ss se ce	v ve	z zz se s	sh	(**th**)	ng (**nk**)

b bb	c k ck	d dd	g gg	h	j g ge	p pp	qu	t tt	w wh	x	y	ch tch

Each box contains one sound but sometimes more than one grapheme.
*Focus graphemes for this story are **circled**.*

Vowels

Ask children to say the sounds in and out of order.

a	e ea	i	o	u	ay	ee y	**igh** i	ow o
at	hen	in	on	up	day	see	high	blow

oo	oo	ar	or oor ore	air	ir	ou	oy oi
zoo	look	car	for	fair	whirl	shout	boy

Story Green Words

Ask children to read the words first in Fred Talk and then say the word.

flung   knight   fluff   kind   eyes*

Ask children to say the syllables and then read the whole word.

Dann|y   mid|night   moon|light   sett|ee   night|light   day|light

supp|er*   un|der*   be|tween

Ask children to read the root first and then the whole word with the suffix.

frighten → frightened   rush → rushed   spot → spots

cook → cooking

* Challenge Words

Vocabulary Check

Discuss the meaning (as used in the story) after the children have read each word.

	definition:	sentence:
moonlight	the light from a full moon	Bright moonlight.
flung	threw off	I flung back the sheet.
supper	evening meal	She was cooking her supper.
knight	a soldier in metal armour	It was a knight to fight the Bump-a-lump.
nightlight	a lamp	In the knight's head, there was a nightlight.
slid between the sheets	cuddled down into bed	I slid between the sheets and shut my eyes tight.

Red Words

there	watch	small	what
some	of	was	to
watch	you	I've	I'm
all	are	there	school
call	were	said	they

Danny and the Bump-a-lump

Midnight. Bright moonlight.

There was a thing under my bed ...

Aaaaaaagh! Help!

I flung back the sheet and went to find Mum.

She was sitting on the settee, watching "The Highjack" on TV.

Mum: Danny! Back to bed, right away!

Me: But I've got a thing under my bed.

Mum: What is it?

Me: It's a Bump-a-lump.

Mum: What's a Bump-a-lump?

Me: Just a Bump-a-lump.

Mum: Is it there in the daylight, or just in the night?

Me: Just in the night.

Mum: Is it big or small?

I shook my head.

Mum: Is it red, or green, or pink, or ...

I shook my head.

Mum: Tell me, Danny. Have you seen this Bump-a-lump?

Me: No. But it's there, all right.
I'm frightened of it!
Tell it to go away!

Mum: Don't be silly.
Go back to bed.

The next night ...

Bright moonlight,
and there was still a thing under my bed!
Aaaaagh! Help!

I flung back the sheet and
rushed off to find Mum.

She was cooking her supper.

Mum: Danny! Back to bed, right away!

Me: But, Mum, I've got a thing under my bed!

It's a Bump-a-lump!

It's always there, in the night!

It might be big, and it might be small!

It might be red, or green, or pink,

or maybe gold with black spots!

I'm frightened of it!

Tell it to go away!

Mum: What you need is something
to frighten the Bump-a-lump.

The next night ...

Mum stood something next to my bed.
It was a knight. The right kind of knight
for a fight with a Bump-a-lump.
In the knight's head, there was a nightlight.
I slid between the sheets and shut my eyes tight.

Mum: Right! This will send the Bump-a-lump away!
You will be all right tonight.

Me: Thanks, Mum.

Mum: Do you think you can get to sleep?

Me: I might ... I think I might ...

Mum: I'm having a look under the bed ...
That's not a Bump-a-lump!
It's just a bit of fluff!
Goodnight, sleep tight, kiss kiss!

Me: Zzzzz! Zzzzz!

Questions to talk about

Ask children to TTYP each question using 'Fastest finger' (FF) or 'Have a think' (HaT).

p.9 (FF) What does Danny's mum tell him to do?

p.10 (FF) When is the Bump-a-lump there?

p.11 (FF) What does Danny want his mum to do?

p.12 (HaT) What do you think Danny's mum thought when Danny came to find her that night?

p.13 (FF) What does Danny's mum think he needs?

p.14 (FF) What does Mum give Danny to scare the Bump-a-lump?

p.15 (HaT) Why does Mum look under the bed?

Questions to read and answer

(Children complete without your help.)

1. Mum was sitting on **the floor / the settee / the bed**.

2. Danny thinks about the Bump-a-lump **at night / in the daylight**.

3. Mum was **cooking her supper / looking at her book / having a nap**.

4. Mum put **a Bump-a-lump / a teddy / a knight** next to Danny's bed.

5. There was **a bit of fluff / a Bump-a-lump / a bad dog** under the bed.

Speedy Green Words

Ask children to practise reading the words across the rows, down the columns and in and out of order clearly and quickly.

shook	seen	silly	tight
send	tonight	tight	tonight
right	away	night	daylight
just	green	head	frighten
next	thanks	sleep	goodnight